Postcards from a War Zone

by

Ron Whittle

The opinions in this manuscript are those of the
Author and do not reflect any of the positions of the
United States Government. Any resemblance to
anyone on the planet earth is a complete and
utter mistake. This book is the work of nonfiction,
names, characters, places and incidents are a product
of the Author's imagination. It's not always
coincidental that much of the book is written with
others in mind. And you know who you are all
rights reserved

To contact the Author,
send Email to whittle_ron@yahoo.com

Published by Human Error Publishing
Paul Richmond
www.humanerrorpublishing.com
paul@humanerrorpublishing.com

Table of Contents

Forward

I can't remember who started it, it may have been
my father, but I have always referred to myself
as the kid. It may have been because I looked so
young with the fair skin, blond hair and blue eyes.
So you know what the kid did today, sounds like
words my father would have used in the description
of something I did. Believe me, there was a lot I
got into and did. At the time, years ago no one
understood and now that I think about it no one
still does. I'm older now, beyond my retirement
years and you know what the kid did today? Who
would have ever thought the kid would have ever
written a book, least of all poetry but the kid
did. This is book number three and may well be
the most important one. Just as a point of
reference the kid loves to pull practical jokes, he
always has and I doubt that will change before
I die and even then I might leave a gag or two
behind. That's just the way this kid was and still
is.

So the saga of the kid continues in this next book.
The kid was sent off to war by the
government that needed more fodder for the many
skirmishes and battles in Vietnam. By some great
miracle the kid survived and somehow managed to
keep some resemblance of sanity. It took a great
many years to forgive myself for the actions the
kid took, when survival took center stage. But
what may have hurt even more was not having any-
one I could talk to about it afterwards.

I believe after all these years the kid found a
voice and a means to talk about it. It's about
love and war, an age old story with a modern
twist.

And this part of the story begins here.

Acknowledgements

This is for all my brothers
I served with, fought with
and bled with
It's too numerous
to name all of you
Some of you I will never
remember your names
but I will always have
your face in my memories
And to Lynne
who gave me comfort
when there wasn't any
to be had anywhere
You gave me a place to hide
in the shelter of your arms
even though we had no idea
where either of us was at the time

The long and short of war
in a few brief words
of my own

Offering up prayers while we waited
for anyone to lower their weapons
They did not and had to die
and did so with all honor as combatants
I hated them for what they represented
and what they did to me
and put me through
but death was swift and respectful

They have come to represent
all that I have lost
all that was taken from me
and all that I never had
and I still hate them

There is no forgiveness left in me
only the regret I was the one
who had to do it

1968, 1969, and part of 1970

For what it's worth

Once, I bought a portable typewriter just be-
fore going to war. I used it whenever I could
to document what I saw, did and felt. It was
my only relief from the strains of war, never
thinking any of my writing would ever be pub-
lished.

A prayer to go home on

God give me the strength
to live and love again
despite all my scars
I want to be brave enough
to live boldly
in spite of the potential grief
I must face
Sleep comes so hard
and I'm so tired of being beaten
with dreams that are all too real
Give me some place
to lay my weary head
free from the mares of the night
that haunt me
Grant me the reason
to go on
when I feel I have none

Lynne

It's amazing what I remember
about yesterday
and how much I already want to
forget about today

Ron

Free
War Zone

I'm not sure where I am today
and I lost track of the date
Medivac
I Corp
South Vietnam

Free
War Zone

Back at China beach for awhile
just outside of DaNang
1969
grounded because of the rain

Lynne

You know we wouldn't be strangers
anymore
if you'd just write and say hi
I've thought so much about you
today I'm exhausted. Sleep is pre-
cious when you can get it, the
rocket attacks come every night

Me

Free
War Zone

June 1969
USS IWO JIMA LPH 2
off the coast of DaNang

Lynne

I'm sure not the big door prize am I
We crashed again today, I was lucky
again. I don't think I have it in
me to do it again. Got rescued by
another flight crew. I'm a little
banged up and in sick bay for a day
or two

Me

PS. real food for a change

Free
War Zone

June 1969
I Corp
China beach
South Vietnam

Lynne

Got our new bird today. I can't
get by without telling you that
love does some pretty stupid
things. I'm living proof of that,
huh!

Me

Free
War Zone

July 1969
I Corp
Da Nang. South Vietnam

Mom

I'm well and okay, the rainy season
is just starting here. They say it
will rain for weeks at a time. I
don't think it could be anymore
humid. Our flight time will be
somewhat limited with the onset of
rain. Even though my helicopter
is all weather, wind and heavy rain
will keep us grounded. I'll write
more when we stop flying.

Ron

Free
War Zone

July 1969
I Corp
China Beach,
South Vietnam

Little Sis

Keep sending me the peanuts cartoon
strips. They crack me up. Thanks
for the socks I needed them pretty
badly. The guys and I
chowed down on the cookies, thank
you, we needed that

Ron

Free
War Zone

July 1969
I Corp
China Beach,
South Vietnam

Dad

Be watching for a fairly large
package coming from here. I bought
you a 5 string banjo, I remembered
you always wanted one. Have fun
with it. I got it through the Navy
Exchange.

Ron

Free
War Zone

NO

You're Drunk
NO
No no
Absolutely no
Most definitely not
Don't be ridiculous
Why are you calling me drunk
I mean
Who would name their kid drunk

Property of the enlisted men's club in DaNang

I'm a man

I'm a man
and have been for some time now
I was forced into manhood
by a war I didn't believe in
I didn't want to be a grown-up
I was a boy with a dream
but the gun in my hands
told me otherwise
I am consumed and appalled
by what I have seen and done
I have come to terms
with my nightmares
and now
Now that I'm an old man
I dream of a boy

of a boy that became a man
long before he was ready

There are no filling stations here

I'm in a loss of direction
and feel totally vulnerable
I'm finding what I want is impossible
When I don't know what I really need
it seems I only know what I have words
for
at least that's what
my heart is telling me
I'm lost in the rush hour traffic in
my mind
with no road maps to set me free

Free
War Zone

August 1969
I Corp
DaNang, South Vietnam

Lynne

There are no churches here, at least none
that
I would take my hat off for. Even God
is afraid to walk where I've been.

Me

Lynne

I smashed our hootch's mirror today. I
can't stand looking at what I have become.

Me

August 1969
I Corp
China Beach, South Vietnam

Free
War Zone

Yesterday is gone

I was just a helicopter doggie
No friends
No family
Only the air crew
We depended on each other
to do our jobs
our lives depended on that
Though it was good to be on the ground
there was more excitement in the air
We did everything together
and even on the ground we talked
like we did in the air, I mean
" What the fuck over"
I must admit I both loved it
and hated it
but I am glad that it is over
It was a very lonely time in my life
It was a time for battle wounds and scars
and things we rarely talk about
I'm glad I made it home
but my thoughts go out to those who didn't
and to a love I had to leave behind
I cry from time to time
when I think of things I had to do
it's hard not to

The easy chair

It's easy to talk about it
sitting in my easy chair
I'm not sure I want to share it
just yet anyway
I mean I need to think about it some
before I let the words
slip from my tongue

We all say things we don't mean
and sometimes mean things we didn't say

I have an affliction for
not reading between the lines
or understating the obvious
or distorting a vision

The truth lies somewhere between
how it's presented
and what is heard
I want you to understand me
and where I have come from
before I say what I feel
and speak from my heart

Free
War Zone

For Linda
July 1969
China Beach, South Vietnam

Drifting on a dream

Behind my closed eyelids
I'm drifting on a dream I've created
somewhere
Tiptoeing on the technicolor horizon
Directing the symphony of the setting sun
and listening to the crickets in stereo

I'm afraid to open my eyes
to find another night of empty arms
I know you're there
I can smell your perfume
and taste your lips of love

But how can I trust lonely arms
that have mistaken pillows
for the warmth of you being near

Thinking of yesterday

In this the day of automation
draught beer and lollypops
I find myself
Filing past tombstones of old thought
Examining the scars of wounds healed
and just generally thinking of yesterday
But time and time again
one wound always reopens
to bring me misery in the highest degree
I tried to forget
but I can't pretend forever
It wasn't lost time I shared with you
but an experience I could never forget

Free
War Zone

For Linda
July 1969
South Vietnam

For Linda
August 1969
China Beach, South Vietnam

Wild as the wind

I cannot pretend you didn't
touch the depths of my soul
The knee buckling weight
of what I have done
and the promises I have broken

I'm blinded by the light of reason
my thoughts as wild as the wind
and it's a matter of the truth
in the closed windows of my mind
If you listen
you can hear the changing of the tide

I'm caught in a groove
and my fears won't subside
The doubt shadow hangs over me
The burden of nightly tears
before sleep settles in

So I can dream and pretend
I hadn't hurt you and
what could have been

For Linda
August 1969
China Beach, South Vietnam

Your door was open

It's easy for dreamers like me
to feel the way that I do
My thoughts
like many different types of clouds
drift on by
Someone once told me
my head was in the clouds

I tried to prove them wrong
It wasn't easy you know
as I drifted on by

Your door was open
and we locked eye to eye
I miss the touch of love
I tried to say

But then clouds don't speak
and lovers don't cry

As I remember it

Free War Zone

In 1969 I was one of 543 thousand
American troops in South Vietnam
At that particular time I was
servicing the 3rd Marine division consisting
of 5 Marine battalions in the early months
of 1969 in the Quang Tri province area. My
squadron was called "The Hounds of Hell," we
were one of the few that flew night ops. My
duties were many as crew chief
Among other things I commanded a fifty
calibre machine gun
out of the crew cabin door.

The hounds of hell bark again

Sooner or later we will stop
chasing the moon
and come out in the broad daylight
but until that happens
The night provides cover
and the darkness swallows us whole
Until we decide when and where
to make an appearance
Oh, you may hear us coming
it's when you see us
that's when the game changes
The night is mine
and I own it and I rule it
and you are the fodder
the night provides
for my weapon and me   1.25.18

Satisfaction guaranteed late in 1969

Free
War Zone

Like war drums
and like a warning
they hear my rotors beat
they hear me coming
but they know not
which direction
They only know
I am among them
and death follows
me into the night
and the red rains down
hell upon them

1969
South Vietnam

The sun is setting for many of us now

Free
War Zone

April 1969
I Corp
DaNang South Vietnam

Lynne

Sometimes I scare myself as to how un-
caring
I have become and how little these peo-
ple mean to me anymore.

Ron

Free
War Zone

May 1969
I corp
DaNang South Vietnam

Lynne

Some days I feel so beat up. It's hard
to find a reason to keep going. If
it wasn't for you I don't know what I
would do. I feel like I have nothing
left to hang onto.

Me

Free
War Zone

June 1969
I corp
China Beach
South Vietnam

Lynne

We got in a dog fight today, it was
bad. We were no more than a slow
flying target for anyone with a rifle.
It was a bumpy ride back, we had the
tip of one blade of our rotor shot off.

Ron

Distant drums

A long list of hidden reasons
and lost chances to reveal them
of things that should have been said
that obviously were not
The trigger upon which my finger rests
and a war that has eaten a hole
through the flesh and bone
to my very soul
and what has been permanently etched in
my mind
the fear, the elation, the bleeding and
dying alone
Wrestling with these dark thoughts and
memories
the Angels and I
and how it's all connected
life before and after the war
and how I should have cried
but could not
Sometimes the silence echos in the empty
void
of the lingering past
and I put aside the present
as the distant drums of war pound out
the call of duty once again
for the gun and I

Blue

How can that be
that you're the one
who quenches all the thirst in me
And there are too many reasons
why I shouldn't be thinking of you
too much time and distance in
the space we once shared
but your eyes
they're just so blue
I can't stop thinking about those eyes
they're too damned blue

12.11.17
Worcester, Ma.

Because this is who we were

The wings of angels
soar above in green helicopters
and the hounds of hell bark
The rotors thump
and out of the clouds
comes death
and death's name is mine
Reward comes with risk
that we once took
and there is no winning
if you cling to safety
When war becomes personal
there is no compromise
for whom the dice roll
God's damned
pay the price on both sides
and the only thing conditional
is the living and the dying
loading and reloading
and not much changes
in the face of war
We can not forget because
we are the only ones who know
what we weren't
The hounds are restless tonight
And I come in their name
For I am the third horseman
cloaked in black
and death is my name

12.11.17 Worcester, Ma.

You know,
I almost fell in love with December

It's always been in the numbers
The number of people we have loved
The number of people who loved you
The number of people you told I love you
The number of people who told you they
love you
The number of people who couldn't say it
The number of people who know
The number of times I have regretted not
saying it
I only know of one for sure
and through all the numbers
My mouth will always hold the taste
of your two lips the last time I touched
them
and yes, I have loved you by the
numbers

12.12.17
Worcester, Ma.

No date
nor a title
nor even where it was written

I have never been able
to replace your touch and heart
to become my own again
Too many maybes
one too many could have beens
way too many at leasts
It's all too much like poetic kindness
What I felt was the softness
of your rose
What I showed them was your blood
on the thorns
We weren't born knowing how to walk
but we have learned how
I still trip over you
even after all these years
We weren't born knowing how to talk
but we have learned how
and over the course of time I have said
a lot
but the most important thing
I never said, I love you

I have never believed in signs
but I do believe in warnings

Yes it's true
almost every sentence of mine
starts off with your name
The thing of it is
your name is always in my mouth
just waiting for me to open it
and it slips out
before I can say anything else
It's been so long since
we actually said anything
to one another
I suppose that it doesn't matter
I talk to you all the time anyway
I don't think you can hear me
but it still gives me comfort
in the dead of the night
When I need it the most
and by some miracle
in the morning my outlook
on life has changed
somewhat
I'm not as angry as I was
the night before
it's that time in the morning
when I can still laugh
to cover up the pain

February 1969 - For Lynne
I Corp DaNang, South Vietnam

The hollow feeling of knowing it's all over
and now paying the price of survival

Free War Zone

In the final months of the war for me
I became very hardened and cold
when put on the spot
There was always the hands of faith around
A presence always just behind us
waiting for us to notice
to believe right now scares the hell out of me
The dirt runs deep with red
and the Angels circle overhead
at every cry for a medic
The smell of burning hurts the very air we breathe
and the vulgar words we speak tear at the flesh of
our enemy
Nothing is going to hurt as good as this
even if I am the only one
who brings swift retaliatory death to those
that would harm or maim or kill me
And nothing sells fear like the wounded
screaming in agony and pain
that I am more than happy to inflict it
upon my enemy
Even though, death tastes odd upon my tongue
The gaping jaws of the cruelty in war
seek out yet another pound of flesh
that someday I will have to pay for
and I wonder to whom
isn't it strange the absence of God

12.12.17
Worcester, Ma.

I've heard it said that everyone has a
chapter in their life they do not read
out loud

Free
War Zone

I may have walked out
of the best day of my life
And I'll never know
if that could have ever been true
Just for the record
every time I was with you
it felt like the first time
and every time your lips touched mine
I didn't want it to end
I will always be
somewhere between
the words I have written about you
and those I haven't
even thought of yet
And I am so afraid I built
a castle in the sand
that would be washed away at high tide
I've been back to that beach
in my mind and dreams
many times and there are still
remnants of walls, towers and moats
standing
waiting for my return

for Lynne   June 1969
China Beach
South Vietnam

The war and I have nothing in common

Sometimes in life we have to do things
we really don't want to
but once we get started
then we have to live with it
breathe with it
eat with it
and if necessary die with it
Such are the ways of being a Warrior
then we move on doing what must be done
with no looking back
It's too late for second guessing at that
point
You'll have plenty of time later on in
life
to try and reason it out
if it doesn't eat you alive first

12.13.17
Worcester, Ma.

Only the damned are unafraid
That's affirm Hotel three four over

The walking damned
are the lucky ones
they are still bleeding
we deliver them to hell
and expect to pick the squad up
or parts of them
to deliver them back
to their mothers
The days too short
and the nights too long
sleep is for the dead
Perimeters are deep and wide
LZ nearly nonexistent
and under constant fire
We extract them
as best as we can
we do what we do
because we want to
With automatic weapons
and machine guns
blazing a means out
hearts beating and bleeding
after a momentary rise
to gain altitude
our return flight begins
under heavy fire
The wounded are bandaged

and the extent of their wounds
radioed ahead

Alpha Mike Foxtrot over

This is based on a true event that happened
on a rescue mission off a fire base
north and west of DaNang July 1969
I never met guys braver than these
men. I honor them with only the part of
the story in which I was involved.

I must allow myself to feel life
while I'm still in it

There is nothing quite as painful
as grieving for the living
The ones that mean so much to you
If it was a true love
it will be instantly
swept back into the moment
it was before
with the same wonder and hope
Real connection
Real love lives on forever
Neither time
nor distance
nor even a war
can destroy that

For Lynne
March 1969
I Corp
DaNang, South Vietnam

Sometimes you just have
to make it happen

I tried so hard to forget
when I came home
That's the funny thing about war
only now do I remember
how I prayed
for the things I have now
It's only today
that I give thanks
for what I have
and cry for those
who lost everything

12.16.17
Worcester, Ma.

Free
War Zone

Many of you may have seen
the photographs of us,
too few got the picture

While I was in Vietnam
I and thousands of others
like me
needed a hero
to look up to
Then I realized one day
all of us
in this war
are the heroes,
no matter what
the people back home
thought of us
We didn't start
this damned war
and I'll be damned
we are not going to
lose it on my watch
To this day
I salute all my comrades
in arms and welcome
them home
We may have inadvertently
saved each other's lives
by our actions
and not known it

12.16.17
Worcester, Ma.

Free
War Zone

In a place not called home

I'm not sure
where home is anymore
It's just a shadow
of a time that was
of faded glory
and will never be again
So what's the point
of picking up the pieces
Life as we knew it
will never be the same
Yesterday we understood
there would be no tomorrow
Tomorrow is for dreamers
and lovers
and not for us the ones
who carry the weight
of living and dying
in a place
not called home

1969
South Vietnam

I know this to be true

Free
War Zone

There are some things in this life
that scare the hell out of me
and they take no physical form
to speak of such as
thoughts
words
love
lust
fear
loneliness
heartbreak
They are only some of the things we feel
but can never touch
and once touched by the feeling
life as we once knew it
has changed forever

12.15.17
Worcester, Ma.

Free
War Zone

12.29.17
Worcester, Ma.

And that is the truth of the matter

Lynne you asked me,
"Where was the last time we kissed ?"
I told you, "I think it was in DaNang".
You said, "you never went to Vietnam".
I thought for a moment and said
"That doesn't mean we didn't kiss there".
You said, "Look, I know I've never been there".
Well, I was there and I'm pretty sure
we danced in one of the dance halls.
I know I held onto to you for dear life
and would have never let you go home
without giving you a kiss. goodbye

By the dawn's early light

My past called me again
this morning
I hung up twice
but the third time
I answered
I'm sorry I did
fear and rage took me back
to where I did not
want to go
I was so frightened for the boy
that was me
that had to relive
the times he wishes to forget
Rage kicked in
after I hung up the phone
I don't bleed as much
as I used to
but the bruises
hang on for awhile

12.29.17
Worcester, Ma.

Over time, you learn how to dance the PTSD
dance

Listen, I did not endure all those hardships
to be pitied at the finish line of life
I made it home from the war
and I'm alive
and I'm doing reasonably well staying that way
even though some days I have my doubts
The pain comes and goes
but at least I am not an open wound anymore
It's tiring bleeding all over the place
when the rest of the world does not
Besides, peace will come soon enough
under the stone with my name on it

7.25.17
Worcester, Ma.

Free
War Zone

53

There are no accidents on this road
tonight

Free
War Zone

You can only kill someone or something
so many times no matter
how much you hate them or it
At first it wasn't personal
until you watched a friend die
and then another
and another
Then it becomes a personal thing
that consumes you
It eats you up
It happens so slowly
Slow enough
you don't even recognize it
for doing so
Until the day you cross
that invisible line
When there are not enough
bullets to fire
to kill what is already dead

God forgive me

1.1.18
Worcester, Ma.

Finding the end of the circle

Free War Zone

The stranger in the dark said
we don't need you
and all your broken parts
I was barely sober
the entire last two years in school
I couldn't live with myself
with what I had done
and it wasn't until I couldn't drink anymore
Did the pain really hit me
Did I finally realize what I had done
And someone put a gun in my hands
and said, go over there son and kill
your country needs you
The daily grind of death and more death
in between the wounds that bled
and the sobering thoughts
of trying to live within myself
I was looking for some kind of normalcy
that would not be found by anyone
in this hell hole
I didn't pray very often
but when I did, I prayed not for sympathy
but prayed for you more than not
I found a voice in of all places
the middle of a fire fight
Square one was the only place that was real
Square one is where it all began
and strangely enough
is ending up there as well

1.2.18   Worcester, Ma.

My New Year's resolution for 1970
to see everything in focus

I woke up to a new year
another time
another day
I'm the same
well maybe not
but the war still rages
death doesn't die
the wounded still bleed
and bullets don't stop
just because it's
New Year's day
It went from 1969 to 1970
and I feel older
than my years
and there is not much
to celebrate here
other than to live
one more day

Nothing promised
Nothing taken
Nothing gained

Vietnam

Free
War Zone

1.2.18
Worcester, Ma.

I'm never right
but when I'm wrong

We were soldiers then
now trapped
in human bone
wrapped in flesh
A prison of sorts
A monster
A savior
The wounded
The dying
The dead of heart
Locked up
trapped in our misery
Who knows better
the taste of blood
than the one
who lets it

57

Looking back through my broken windows

My feelings for you
had been too real
alive and burned
setting flame to anything
that it touched
but you had never felt the heat
nor saw the flames
before the crash and burn
The scars run deep
and there are wounds that still bleed
when touched or disturbed
Please don't hate me
for what I can not control
I can only thank God
for giving me what
little time I had with you
and all the memories
that kept me alive
in the shear desperation
of a moment in time
when your love
came shining through
the dark cloud covered skies of war
to find me
when I needed someone
the most

12.30.17 Worcester, Ma.   Remembering Vietnam
Lynne, I hope this explains some of my early
poetry. I want you to understand why you will
always be in my heart. I am so thankful you
found someone who loves you as much as I did.

Where butterflies once fluttered

Don't ever feel sorry
for what you did for me
for you gave me something
I would never have had
The goodness within you
will stay with me
my entire life
You gave me hope
when there was none
You gave me reason
when there wasn't any
You put the spark
in my heart
that allowed me to love
How could I ever
forget that

For Lynne
March 1968
Da Nang, South Vietnam

Free
War Zone

12.17.17
Worcester, Ma.

You don't make me cookies
anymore

Just because it had ended for me
didn't mean it was over
The nightmares persisted
long after I was gone
and on occasion
I still have them
We were one of many
until we came home
when I became I again
Alone
The road home
is long and wide
and I've never been too sure
I would ever get there
on my own

Free
War Zone

1.5.18
Worcester, Ma.

A Veteran's calling card

It still burns within me
The feeling for now hides
but is not far from the surface
it is still here, I can hear it
and some days it still calls my name
some days not so much
but it does come calling
no matter how much
I try not to pay attention to it

Searching for what's left of me

We need to heal the way we need to heal
each of us is different in that process
it's the only way to find the open door

Some need more help than others
Some need no help at all
Some never will try
others will never have the chance
Some have hid it well
Some pretend it never happened
Some struggle in the darkness
and others remember the sunshine

I choose to find the sunshine
and try to hang onto the warmth
rather than go back to the darkness

1.6.18
Worcester, Ma.

All of us came back with some form
of PTSD, some more so than others.

Your grace grips my pen

Free
War Zone

I had to live with
all the different sounds
in my heart
as well as the sounds of
regret pumping
through my veins
I am that guy
Who can write the words
and why do we die
and lie in a box
only to be buried
deep in the ground
All I ask of you
In the end
at least
care enough
or just a little
to give me some reason
to go on living
and believing
IF there is an eternity
I am the remains
of my identity
lost in the carnage
of war
and I couldn't live with
yet another
incomplete fairytale

VIETNAM in a another place another time

You will never come back from loving an angel

Free
War Zone

We were the
fear and pain and love
in a room filled with treasures
trying to find one another
and the meaning of love
Hugs and kisses that threaten
to merge our bodies into one
Then the coming of the rain
and the slow wringing out of
ourselves individually
Remnants of the storm that passed
hang heavy in the air
amid the shaking and quivering flesh
and puddles of tears from
behind both sides of the fence
The star in my pocket
mounted on a ring of gold
burns my hand and leg
and I have lost all sense of direction
and lost my purpose in life
and what is it supposed to be
other than loving her forever
I don't know and may never
Thunder shakes the ground
upon which I walk
and I can find no meaning left
and how do I continue on without her
Hanging my head in shame
How does a mortal
break the heart of an angel
sent to save him from himself

Vietnam

You were my favorite feeling
I guess I felt too much

Somewhere in between
the sunset and sunrise
the stars are beautiful tonight
How can you be afraid of the darkness
when I have more reason than you
to be fearful
I said your name out loud today
I haven't done that in a long time
and your name tasted like heaven
so I said it over and over again

Once on a night much like this one
lying on my belly in the
blood soaked stench of dirt
My heartbeat kept me alive
Your heartbeat lets me keep on living
Our heartbeats gave me reason to live
and I loved you in silence
too afraid to move in the darkness
for fear of what would come next

Vietnam

Wolves wish too

All I want is to stand out in all that I
endeavor
I want to do the things I want to do
not what someone else tells me I should do
I'm not good at following the rules
I am me and I'm unique
and have always been that way
I think you knew that
One summer we grew up and apart
but the passion and love never left
it's always just a skin depth away
from resurfacing again
Understand I am not as strong
as I would appear to be
Wolves wish to be cherished too
You were the key to my life
even though I changed all my locks
I let you in every time you knocked
Tomorrow is only a page away
love is not an escape
and love is more than
an orgasmic toe curling event
it is how we found ourselves
in the throws of passion
That was another time and place
on a different page in the book of life
I've been busy counting seeds
and failed to realize I grew a garden
and sometimes you taste just like regret

I remember how
my hands slid to your waist
and how I crashed on your curves
There was no one there to rescue me
then
or ever

For Lynne
Vietnam 1969

Free
War Zone

1.22.18
Worcester, Ma.

As I see it on any given day

you
can run
through the woods
once
maybe
twice
but to try
over and over again
sooner
or later
I'm gonna get ya
in my sights

This is my playground

I am the darkness
I own the night
I am up
I am down
I am north and south
and east and west
I wear the night
like a cheap jungle green jacket
You may hear
the thump of the rotors
It is useless to hide
I will find you
I am death
and I am very good
at what I do

Free
War Zone

1969
Vietnam

To my enemy
We see each other eye to eye

In the end
we may both know each other
with better familiarity
than we do ourselves
We do what we do
because it's what we do
and I must confess
I don't like you
and it's not just because
I do it better
than you
It's because of what
you made me become

Free
War Zone

1969
Danang, South Vietnam

Free
War Zone

1969
Danang, South Vietnam

The bruised pages of a combat manual

This might have been a curse
or it might be karma
biting at my ass
Hell was empty
and in need of some souls
but I will not
give it mine willingly
and I offer no apologies

Nineteen and frighten

I was once in the business of war
Death and dismemberment
was my business
and business was good
Far better in those days than today
and I was even better at what I did
than most
and those that knew me
didn't for very long
I was that good
or bad depending on your point of view
that didn't last that long
My shadow still lingers over
those now empty battlefields
as an ever constant reminder
of when I took up residence there
and the only one who knew my name
will be the one I'm answerable to
for what I have done

1.15.18
Worcester, Ma.

Without letters or intention

Sometimes I'm surprised anyone
can relate to anything
I say or write about the war
I forget I wasn't the only one over there
so I have to remind myself
I wasn't the only one to bleed
I forget I was one of the lucky ones
who didn't die there
I forget I wasn't the only one
who shot not only in self defense
but in anger
I don't know why I'm surprised
that friends had to die
I mean that's the nature of war
some of us bled
and others of us had to die
in order for it to be called a war

1.13.18
Worcester, Ma.

The exhibitionist

Free
War Zone

It was on a Tuesday
though it might not have been
it could have been any day of the week
as one day bled into the next
just as one week
was the same as any other
The only difference was
how close we came to dying
Some days were worse than others
and what kind of risks
we were required to take
High risk rescues were our specialty
we did what others could not
not that we were any braver
than anyone else
In fact we may have been more scared
than anyone else
which may have made us
a more cohesive air crew
we covered each other's six
pretty well
Shooting my gun
I yell out the door
Tag you're it
and I owe them
no further explanation
but some sons of bitches
require multiple tags
because they do not believe
they are out of the game
until I assure them they are

4.5.18
Worcester, Ma.

Nobody ever tells you what it's
like when they die

There have been times
when I didn't know
the stranger in my skin
When nothing made any sense
and here I am doing
what I was trained to do
To remove those that
do not agree
with my government's stance
I am given the implements
of death and destruction
and told to go do what I do best
Rape and pillage a foreign land
I have questions
but no one to answer them
and it seems as though
there is always another ocean to cross
and another cross to bear
another life to take
And I wonder
when is this all going to end

1.2 3.18
Worcester, Ma.

Free
War Zone

Midnight confessional

Free
War Zone

Something I saw this night
out of my helicopter door
left me quaking in my boots amid
the blazing guns and exploding rounds
You came out of the dark
and into my sights
in that glorious hallelujah moment
when I watched you in slow motion
try to rush me firing your gun
I shot you and you stumbled to the
ground
and somewhere in my mind
a momentary thought
neither friend but rather foe
anyone one that brave
deserved to live
and who am I to play God
but the chatter of my gun
knew better and did
exactly what it was supposed to do

1.15.18
Worcester, Ma.

Afraid of nothing for I already have wings

Wild is the music
of the empty brass shell casings
bouncing off the metal deck
of the helicopter floor
I thirst for that friendly sound
The chug and thud
The intimacy only I know
of reloading and cocking the bolt
The orgasmic pleasure
of pulling the trigger
The rush of adrenaline
the vibrations up the arms and chest
and spitting fire out the barrel
The emotional relief of
profane language
and the lingering sillage
of burnt gunpowder
in the crew cabin
and relaxation does not come
for this old bird
until it rests on its own pad
ready for the last flight

1.13.18
Worcester, Ma.

Free
War Zone

1.14.18
Worcester, Ma

Walking with a big stick

I have lived within the words
I could not write
Sometimes in the military
I never had much certainty
with anything
Until I caught you in my sights
and then I was quite certain
of what would happen next
I may not have been
the baddest ass in the valley
but I was damned
close to it

The roar of distant thunder

I used you for so many days
as a crutch
when things wouldn't go well
You helped me over some pretty rough
times
when death surrounded me
and I hid in your warm embrace
I wouldn't blame you
for not understanding
Sometimes, I didn't either
You never knew it but I carried
your picture with me
in my breast pocket
until the heat and humidity
destroyed it
I cried that night
because I finally thought
it was over and I'd never
make it home
All I had was my empty pockets
and a memory
I wouldn't let fade away
as it was the only thing
I owned
that they couldn't take away from me

The shadow

The weight of your shadow
carries heavy on my back
I took that from you
I took the life from your shadow
No one else knows it is there
but I do
you have no use for it anymore
your body is dead and gone
and your shadow
carries heavy on my back
and weighs heavy on my mind
I see it in my dreams
and it's never far from me
no more than an arm's reach
just so I don't forget
and it forces me to remember
  what I have done
and what the call to war can do

Answering for the sins of yesterday

The war is
branded on my skin
and etched in my mind
Fresh are the smells
of sweat and blood
My ears still ring
from daily gun fire
The burns on my hands
and arms
from ejected shell casings
are a constant reminder
of the lives I have taken
and I can never be
who I used to be
I can only be
what I have become

The sun is setting for many of us now

Sure, I suppose you could call
all of us broken Angels
But the truth is
the sheer weight and responsibilities
may have caused us to bend
but I can tell you for sure
we have not broken
Sure we may have come home
different than before we left
and some may be very angry
while others of us would appear
to be okay and normal
I assure you, we are not
We are anything but
okay and normal
We have been altered by what we
have seen and done
our future shaped
by those who we stood shoulder
to shoulder with
We lived, breathed, bled and died together
We are each others brother and keeper
United we stood
unwavering and unbeaten
and the flag under which we sailed
is what holds us together
and will forever
We will always reserve the right
to wear our emotions on our sleeves

along with our tears
for those that did not make it home
and for the families that had to bury them
There is only one tombstone for us now
and it lays in a field
in Washington DC
with its list of names of heroes
that grows with every passing day

1.21.18
Worcester, Ma.

Free War Zone

By killing someone does that mean you take
over their place in the universe

I sit and type
as I did in my hootch
writing what I have dreamt and done
much like I did with my machine gun
during the days of war
The words come hard, fast and furious
just as the bullets did from my gun
Some words so vile
they could conceivably take a life
and yet I owe no apology for them
nor the bullets from the barrel of my gun

8.2.18
Worcester, Ma.

Free
War Zone

January 1969
I Corp
Just outside of
DaNang, South Vietnam

Hi Lynne

How are you?
Lovely DaNang
I'm still breathing
Can't say I wish
you were here
tho' I wish I was there
Rain with intermittent
bleeding
Bye

Me

Free
War Zone

5.12.69
I Corp
Somewhere
in South Vietnam

Lynne

What I really meant when I said
These memories are ones
that once kissed this mouth
This could have been a card from me
the words are from the heart
but the signature is not mine

Me

Free
War Zone

Somewhere in country
on a hilltop
February, 1969
I Corp
South Vietnam

Lynne

Nothing from you again today
How can we write each other
when neither of us knows where
the other is

Me

Free
War Zone

February 1969
I Corp
in a field hospital
outside of
Hue, South Vietnam

Lynne

The Corpsman said this is gonna hurt
but you'll be all right
it's only a flesh wound
For a flesh wound I sure bled a lot

Me

The dead of night, I know a lot about that

Free
War Zone

9.9.17
Worcester, Ma.

In love we find out who we want to be with
In war we find out who we are
and what we might have been with the one we
loved
I think about you
and wonder if you're okay
on the days that I am not
I think about you
and the distance between us
and the life that will never be
I think about you

no really
I - I think about you

a lot

You saved me in ways you may never understand

Free
War Zone
The military is the introduction
of how to make the other person bleed worse
or preferably introduce them to death
That's war talk
and war is only fascinating
to those who haven't been there
The aftermath is living with what
you had to do to stay alive
and bandaids over open
wounds are mere child's play
What shields one
may not shield the other
and such is the nature of war
As one man's prayer
is oh so different than another's
and how do I tell you I love you more now
than ever before
and I'm not sure any of
this will make sense to you
or is this just mental distress on my part
and anyone who says
they didn't cry at some point is a liar
and what is by far more fearful
is when you can no longer cry
not even for yourself
When death separates itself from life
and is no longer an entity to be feared
it becomes just another fact of
living in combat It's because
you do what you do because it's what you do
in the moments of self preservation
and not wanting to die
with I love you on your lips

9.10.17
Worcester, Ma.

There I was

There was a time
when I thought
I would never write again
I had lost the magic
and the will to see
with my mind
There was a time when the stars
were man-made
and tore into heaven
on the darkest of nights
to illuminate the field of death
and dismemberment
and there was a time when
Words became my anchor
and the ink that had not dried
after so many years
I could finally open my eyes
to read what I had written
in the darkness
of backed in corners
There is a certain fear
in remembering the feelings
and thoughts of those days
that I do not wish to reopen
the old letters of passion
that I did not send
and I still do not know how
to convey what I was feeling
in those days of the darkest of nights
When love and war
were only inches apart

Free
War Zone

7.17.17
Worcester, Ma.

No civility here in the bush

Okay so I'm not the
model of decorum anymore
I like I might have been at one time
My modesty left along with my
propriety and morality
within my efforts in the war
There was no time for modesty
only a time for living and dying
and loading and reloading
and bleeding and praying
and modesty has no place
on the battlefield
death has seen to that

The portrait of the wolves' lair in two parts

Part one

The wolves of war were hungry in those days
The pieces of me lost to the war
wish to be forgotten
but I still have visions
of talking to your
picture
as though you were standing in front of me
Confessing that it felt so right
when my lips touched yours
and how bad it felt knowing it never would
happen again
I guess when it comes down to it
the words are just empty air
expelled from my lungs

Like the light distorted
through the smudged glass windows of my mind

Part Two

The wolves howled at the light of the moon
and sensed the smell of blood and death
that the war provided them with
I stand with gun in one hand and pen in the other
and I paint a picture of colorless words
in the moments leading up to
the bloodletting
The alumni of this and other such events like it
are survivors like myself
that still fight the fight
and wait, much like I do
for my lips to meet hers, once again

Listening 1969

The sun came up this morning
it found me face up in the sand
hands behind my head
listening   just listening
to the sounds of the sea
waves breaking
gulls squawking
the occasional beach walkers
indistinguishable muffled talk

My eyes are closed with visions of you
Lying here beside me
Smiling like you always do
I'm so afraid to open my eyes
for fear that you won't really be here
The sun lights up your face
your eyes are hidden behind dark sunglasses
the wind gently plays with your hair
you smell like suntan lotion
and taste just like the beach
this is how I remember you
on a hot summer morning so many years ago

If I had ten minutes to go back in time
I'd go back to that beach
to that very moment
and tell you how much I love you
and how lonely my future is going to be
without you
For Lynne
August 1969   I Corp   DaNang, South Vietnam

94

A petal falling off a tattooed flower

Free
War Zone

I was once
in the belly of a bird
and soared
totally unapologetically
completely unencumbered
and pretty much
did what we pleased
with little direction
other than
do what we do best
it was not done fearlessly
but never regretfully
and even then
bad things can happen
and usually do
and not so much
for the bird
she flies freely
and with her wings spread
she attempts to
cover those on the ground
Hotel 34 look for smoke over
North by two clicks over
Roger that
after the Pilot's confirmation
of muzzle flash
Hell comes with me

1.26.18

The moon between us

We were young
and turned the world inside out
We were as beautiful as we loved
it's the same moon between us
as it was before
We were not afraid of the dark
I was in love with the way you looked at me
and for every word for everything said
for every beat of my heart
I burn and yet we can't catch fire
We were young and beautiful
and I loved you so
for every mistake I have made
without chance, what good is choice
your face is on every passing stranger
and I cry when I hear our song
whatever my life was
I wanted to spend it with you
Even today I would gladly
spend my last breath
to be with whatever remaining
part of your soul I could reach
The road home always ends with you
I'm lost so lost without you
and the moon mocks me
as I try to find my way

For Lynne
July 1969
China Beach, South Vietnam

There are no warm blankets for warriors

I was once filled with the changing colors
of life
I ink my blood upon page after page
and read letters from home as I lay with
the many
Yet, alone under the stars of a foreign
land
Overwhelmed by death and love
and I never knew how to sort it all out
A part of me died there
and I am still alive at least a little bit
of me anyway
We share different blankets a world apart
and my thoughts are wrapped in sheets
I will never see but I can feel
You intoxicate me with a string of words
that I write down in prose
and the new day comes with new words
that all say the same thing in different
ways
Living in personal heavens and hells
too afraid to sleep when dreams take me
to the pits of hell or to your front door
The nightmares raped my dreams
where no one could be trusted
and I fear the bodies of the dead I killed
will come back for me
and the time to heal will outlive me
The rules I have had to bend,
it's all too complicated

This living and dying
and loving and hating
and I have to bleed to be set free from
all this
and I need to wash death off of me
I sought the truth and honesty and found
anything but
My body was broken
waking to my insides pulling me apart
and it's ironic that this country bleeds
patriotism
but destroys its law bound by some mis-
guided principles
I should have been there
for your yesterdays
and it's all in the words we say or didn't
say
Love is more than me and you
and when the stars saw
you were one of them
they took you away from me
as I looked to the foreign night sky
in a strange land
I smile at the sight of you

There is always hope as dawn is reborn

I can bleed verse on the pages
but cannot feel the words
let alone see them in the light
of the moon
There is a certain violence
in the midnight sky
that goes with the silence of the stars
and since I tasted the darkness of the
night
and the sting of lead
and the burnt flesh
from the brass shell casings
The darkness of the night
does not frighten me
it's what lays in wait that does
Dawn's broken promise
yields me a prisoner to the night
In dreams you fill all the corners
of my mind
with the eloquent dreams of love past
You stand beside me barefoot
among the green blades of grass
Even though I am fully clothed
in jungle greens
your stare has left me naked
exposed and vulnerable
and I fear the creep of death
that surrounds me
and the thoughts
of what you tasted like

and the softness of your mouth
It was a very confusing time
of love and death
when the thirst of the soil
is only quenched
by the blood of the dead

There is no give up here

Sutured wounds
Dead stacked like cord wood
Helicopters hover
Corpsmen run from body to body
machine guns fire
RPGs explode
Bandaged arms and legs
of men put back in the line of fire
there is no quit here
Heroes are made
the dead forgotten
Blood that was given
lives that were taken
Automatic weapons fire into the night
tracers bounce and sing
flares light the darkness
Enemy sighted
and gunned down
Mortars rain down hell on earth
death surrounds us
we never give in
and what's the cause
Pull back the perimeters
then stand your ground
there is no give up here
by the first morning light
the only thing left was those of us
who could be counted
and a surrealistic pock marked moonscape

of foliage stripped trees
and the enemy dead
Everything was burned
smoldering, blown up or destroyed
No birds no animals no grass
only dirt
The smell of cordite
and death that hung in the air
Our wounded medevaced
our dead sent home for burial
Mothers and Wives cried
and our young lives
forever altered
never to be the same

Free
War Zone

So where is normal now

I am not the model of decorum
I am the graduate of the school
of badassery, hard knocks
and high explosives
I was and still am not ready
to be held hostage
to my own thoughts and dreams
And it has finally come to this
The day of reckoning
I personally owned a piece of a war zone
and I paid dearly for it
both physically and mentally
There is a rare moment here of reluctance
in my voice
the fluctuation in tone and cracking
gives way to the true feels
I still have today
for the day to day struggle to survive
I managed to survive
though I don't know how or why
It's the why of things
that eats at the soul
For all my left over idiosyncrasies
from the war
you'd think I would have
gotten over it by now
They sent me home and told me to go back
to my normal life
So what is back to normal
I lost normal at the age of nineteen

and how has normal not effected my day
to day life since
I have no idea what normal is anymore
Normal is not a word I use

Such was the night

There is no remedy
for the way I feel
When shouting into the abyss
no longer works
I command the pencil in hand
yet nothing happens
No words can I write
will do justice
for what I have seen and done
They say forgetting
is everything
How does one forget
those desperate days
when life walked the razor's edge
into the middle of the night
There are two kinds of night
in one option
I would not survive
the other
my inner self would have to
bear the cross
forever

Words failed to justify
the thread we weaved

The joy in life
isn't being lost
it's in the possibility
of being found
and by who

So you understand
it was not over
for me
it's still not
The words tattooed
on my skin
is desperation
trying to feel
alive again

Dreaming of a kiss
a sweet embrace
that will never come
and riddled
with bullet holes
Who can save me now

Free
War Zone

Without pain would I have ever known
peace

Who has time to think about the future
Here, there is only the now to live in
Here, there is no tomorrow
only the promise of this minute
and even at that
sometimes
that is even questionable

8.2.18
Worcester, Ma.

The water is wet because God made it so

I mistook my pain for weakness
and yet my pain I suffer with everyday
leads the way for others that depend on me
not to show it
I had to learn my pain does not make me
weak
There is a strength in pain that most will
not know
and only those that shared this war with me
can and will understand

South Vietnam
1969

ALPHA MIKE FOXTROT

Free
War Zone

In the midst of thousands
I stood alone
I bent but didn't break
I cried but didn't sob
I killed and didn't care
I bled while others slept
I slept while others died
I wrote letters never to be mailed
I wrote poems never to be read
I did what I had to
I said goodbye many times
I vomited till I could no more
I cleaned my weapon until my fingers
bled
I watched friends die
I waited for my time
no time to write home
too sick to care
body parts everywhere
Jungle greens with two week's sweat
blood, vomit and urine soaked
and sleeves soaked with tears
and thru it all I had her picture
that I would talk to now and then
K rats and jungle rot
Everything tasted like cordite
or blood or both
that I still can taste today
and the war still rages
though it's some distance away

John Wayne was never found
suspected KIA
Alpha Mike Foxtrot over

5.16.16
Worcester, Ma.

It's almost over

Free War Zone

Until there were bullets
I never knew freedom
Until there was blood
I couldn't see
I didn't kill any babies
but I did fathers
and maybe a few mothers
There are no words
or medals to erase the memory
Only snapshots of a
time that was
that floats around in my head
A drive-in theater of the mind
If you will
A double feature
that never ends

11.3.17
Worcester, Ma.
and sometimes
I Corp
South Vietnam

This was written for a High school
classmate Jimmy Campaniello
who made it home but left his
soul in Vietnam
God bless you Jimmy

Free
War Zone

June 1969
I corp
South Vietnam

Lynne

Even though
it might have looked like it
I am not looking to change
the world one bullet at a time
I'm just trying to save the piece of it
I'm standing on

Me

Free
War Zone

July 1969
I Corp
South Vietnam

Lynne

When I look in a mirror
I have a choice
to either laugh or cry
I choose to laugh
later I will cry if I can

Me

Letters from my Hooch

Free War Zone

The adventures into the night
so dark I can't see your face
I can hear the whispers in your voice
and the warmth of your breath
the touch of your hand
the softness of your body
the wetness of your lips
the urgency in your movement
as the excitement builds and trembles
time moves on though we didn't notice
feelings running wild with passion
and tears running silently down my face
to yet another night without you
my poems offer little protection
from my love loss
but they are my only source of comfort
in this strange land
that only knows war,
dismemberment and death
I am so frightened and confused
I want you more than I ever have
and yet I know that can never be
no matter how much I wish it to be

For Lynne
April 1969
DaNang
South Viet Nam

Lines that will never intersect

The person I was
is the person I think I am
and I don't know the person I'm trying
to be
but this solitary soldier belongs to
the night
and with grit and determination I hang
onto
what I claim as mine
Destiny will never knock on my door
No one will
for who would want to be me
I sleep with someone missing
I left him over there in the war
It's the person I used to be
the person I was
and no one here will miss him
but me

Dangerous curves ahead

Free War Zone

I was danger and she knew it
There would be no saving us
from heartbreak
It would be by my own making
My love was sensing fire in all directions
my thoughts ran wild with passion
I was in love and didn't know the
symptoms
that was the day your eyes told me a
story
I would never forget
the fear I read scared me
Your kisses were my sin
that was written on each page
The book was never bound nor printed
and it ended shortly after the third
chapter
I have written many a verse since then
but not enough for the next chapter
and nothing worthy enough
for you to read
but my heart will write on
as soon as I dry these tears

August 1968
South Vietnam
for Lynne

Kindred spirits come out of the sky

My enemies speak my name
as if it was some kind of curse
for this I am sure
My comrades
on the other hand
don't know my name
but they know a friendly face
when they see one

8.2.18
Worcester, Ma.

Having already faced the fire

I am acutely conscious of my surroundings
This is a place where granite lays
on top of the dead
A place where broken angels lay in rows
in grassy fields
A place where my brothers and friends lay
in forever sleep
I, like them bought a one way ticket
to hell
and now I wrestle with the guilt
of coming home
when the others did not
The graveside flags flap in the wind
and somewhere in the darkness of my gloom
I am reborn, temporarily free from
despair and sorrow
Looking oceanward the tidal creep
soon to be high tide catches my eye
The edge of night is rising
from the depths of Atlantic blue
and I must go on and live my life as they
would want me to
Silently I say although for now
I must go
My Brothers, someday my bones will rest
with you

I have not forgiven them

Free War Zone

It's probably a good thing
you went away from home
before I got back from the war
I was not easy to love anymore
not that you would have
but if you did
I would have hurt you again
not that I would have
wanted to
I was an ex spent shell casing
left over from the war
Hollow, empty and ejected
to the ground
feeling totally used
by the government I loved
and I sacrificed for
I put my life on the line
for a country looking only
for the profit of a few
while my fellow countrymen
turned their backs to me

I just thought you should know

I can say with all honesty
that there were minutes in every hour
that I lost
and somewhere in the war effort
I became a survivor
Perhaps it was on the way home
There are some fights we can never win
and a hundred stories
that need to be told
We need to survive until we know how
We are both survivors
of different types of wars
I recognize you
when I look in the mirror
when I can barely
recognize myself
I hear your voice in type
and more than anything
I just need to hear
that you are loved

6.3.17
Worcester,Ma.

Remembering just how it was

The sky was dappled with damson purple
as the sun sank low on the horizon
It was the season for deciduous trees
to shed their colorful beauty
And a time for nights
       to be longer

The sunset was quick
      leaving only fond memories
of another day past
the New England air was crisp and fresh
but not yet a biting cold
though winter be only around the corner

It was just how I remembered it
it had been a long time
since I was last home
and even a longer time
since I last saw you

Nothing had really changed
      only the dates
The Moon was the same
your eyes are the same
      and your love
as warm as I had dreamed

Written in South Vietnam 1969
for Lynne

So what if

Free
War Zone

Life is full of what ifs
or if I had onlys
the missed opportunities
and chances at fate
the cards we deal ourselves
So what if
I plucked a star from the midnight sky
and named it after you
would you wear it
around your neck
as a token of my love for you
Would you always remember me
for what I am   or was
and what could have been
As it could have been on your finger
If only I hadn't acted so foolishly
I think I will leave it there
so every time you look up at night
no matter where you are
near or far
you will think of me
Your star is looking down at you
reach out and touch it

For Lynne
Aug 1969
China Beach, South Vietnam

On being a warrior and a poet

Medics cleaned up my battle wounds
but nobody could see the trauma
in my head
except me
Nobody felt the sound of pain
or could feel the calm and anger
There was no sense of ending to the war
It goes on and relived in dreams
The peace you thought would
come with acceptance doesn't
and even in these
the last of my dying days
I write the words of a warrior poet
and there never was the choice of being
either, the warrior or the poet
The visions of war still vividly
flashing in my eyes
and writing was merely an exit
for the pain
while the warrior did his duty
with the gun
and the poet did his job with the pen

A story behind every scar

There is a story behind every scar I bare
and for every feeling I have ever felt
Some I wish I could forget
and some long gone from memories
that time stole away
some were very good
others as bad as it can get
and then there are the ones
about the human elements
of love and death
and the struggle to stay alive
or to keep the love experience
from fading into no more than a dream
Scars have a lasting impact
on the psyche
Scars are the way the body
protects the unseen wounds
and the way I remember
your love that was lost
and those lives that I took in the war

The son of hunger

There is a pleasure of my pen in hand
and writing the words from my heart to
mind
The sawdust that raised me
runs deep in my veins
and the common sense my father taught me
protects me
I do not build anymore
but, I repurpose my dreams
and stare at the sky
There is no war in the clouds
and when it comes to the rain
it is like liquid meditation for my mind
But in the distance I can't help but hear
the rumble
and see the dark clouds on the horizon
I want to fly
and be whisked away from here
to be there where you are
Away from this secret war
and today is not the day
I wish to touch heaven
My soul reaches out
into the unknown
where my feet touch the ground
and in that moment it stops raining
and just for a second, I had a vision of
you
I needed to cry

but found I could not
So instead I bled with it
The last kiss of no hope at all
Disregarding the obvious danger
in the position I am in
hidden behind dark trees
almost naked and nearly invisible
I take careful aim
Death is a lonely man
afraid of everyone
but perfectly willing
to kill
to stay alive
and finding I am the man,
that the boy does not know
nor understand
but one he will have to live with

The soles of worn out boots

My soul and spirit are worn from war
and have never completely recovered
from the wounds of the mind,
sight and sound
Forgive me, if I sound trite
for that is not intended
Only the reality of the effects
of being thrown into situations
where it is impossible not to have killed
and human survival instincts protect us
I would like to be able to say
I have come home
but a very large piece of me still lays in
the open battlefield
with many of my comrade at arms
And will only come home upon my passing
Much of my life today is in retrospect
reliving events I have wished to forget
Some days,
I disappear into the words of others
and won't come back until
I'm ready to reappear
completely absorbed
in the literary refrain
of a master wordsmith
Life's puzzles loom
as they linger mesmerizing
Once I was a flower
Now, I'm just another dead leaf

fodder and compost
for the future to feed on
I'm just a soul who lost a love
and there are a thousand reasons
why my heart must be one with hell
Back when we were younger
but felt so much older
you were the only thing that made sense
I don't know, maybe life is too much today
Too many thoughts and impulses
crashing into one another
These words perhaps
should never leave my mouth
but no matter how much I dream about
being in love, you are still gone
Like some kind of esoteric secret
I need to stop feeling like
our last goodbye
was really goodbye
It's the next goodbye that really scares me

We were young once

I am almost certain there
has been no improvement
in my temperament
It's hard to come back from
being someone you didn't want to be
in a place you wanted no part of
War came rushing at us
as high school graduates
we did what we had to do
and saw what we didn't want to see
Too new to life to fully understand
and too early to have it snuffed out
Fear played its hand
and was immediately trumped
by survival instinct
Some had no choice
it was made for them from
the business end
of a barrel of a gun
triggered and sighted by the enemy
With absolute certainty
I can say life has been interfered with
and has forever been altered
changed in ways
some will never understand
Unseen wounds
that break and tear at the spirit
and heart of a young man
The solace he could not find
anywhere he looked

and there is no privacy in bleeding
or leaking life on the field of combat
Survival depends
on the willingness to live
and the determination
to never to give into the call of death
when it dials up your number
The phone is ringing

Don't answer it

Vietnam

Free War Zone

You are the one
that starts the war
I am the bullet
that starts the battle
I am the emptied shell casings
left out on the battlefield
You are the blood
That runs deep into the ground
I am the one
who has to live
with what I have done
I am the one
that carries the lifetime burden
and you are the one
with eternal sleep

Free
War Zone

December, 1968
I Corp
Da Nang, South Vietnam

Lynne

I made a friend here
he gave me courage
when I had none
and fear controlled me
I guess I'll be okay for awhile

Me

Free
War Zone

Lynne

Early November 1968
USS Iwo Jima LPH-2
Westpac
Somewhere in the Pacific

I've never known this type
of darkness before
no lights for thousands of miles
and billions of stars
I never knew before
happy to make their acquaintance

Me

Free
War Zone

Mid November 1968
USS Iwo Jima LPH-2
Westpac
South China Sea

Lynne

They are letting us relax a lit-
tle
before the big push in a couple
of days
it's nerve wracking
sitting around waiting
with nothing to do
but think

Me

Free
War Zone

11.15.17
Worcester, Ma.

Looking for the light switch

We attack under the cover of darkness
and bad things happen
to those that wait
This is the game of proximity
that is played
and the only rule to the game
is win at all costs
So maybe you could tell me
why the night has
such a bad name
and I no longer fear the fear
but for that
which lays in wait

that I cannot see

The questioning of the Warrior in me

Sometimes I wonder what it's like
to see the light again
instead of the ink that spews
across the naked pages
of a writing tablet
The pulse of a well trained
Warrior
runs through my veins
and it's hard to just give that up
I want to know where my
missing pieces are
and is this where the darkness begins
If I am to survive
it will be by my own hands
In me I trust
as God will have nothing to do with this
and I need to know
can my gut stomach this
Have I the wear with all
to do what needs to be done
and then
the war kissed me in a dark room
In the morning light I vomited
when I saw what I had done
When the enemy in your eyes
becomes something less than human
and becomes just another thing to kill
The spilling of their blood
is on your hands and
those that sent you there

Free
War Zone

to do their bidding for them
Are you prepared to live with
or die from your actions
I want to know is my fate
  balanced with the future
that is stained with the blood
of the victims of war
that I may have killed
For those that died
may be the lucky ones
those that live have to live
with their past actions
and a lifetime of nightmares

An empty shell 1969

I feel so different
like I had no heart or soul left
Just an empty shell of a man
wandering from one to another
meaningless relationship
I could never find what I gave up
surrounded by the darkness
overwhelmed with pain
no one feels the loneliness
when no one hears you cry

It all hangs in the balance

If I was to go back there
It would be so different
I know I'd say I miss it
but I wouldn't miss this place
as it is now
I'd miss it as it was then
The camaraderie
The youthful faces
The way time stood still
The fear and elation
the living and dying
The bandaged and bleeding
Living on the razors edge
never knowing if there
would be a tomorrow
And the facing of fear
until it backed down
I'm not sure
I could do that today
I don't have that kind of
confidence in the length of life
that I had back then

1.22.18
Worcester, Ma.

Free
War Zone

Lynne

This morning we went into general quarters
They announced it was not a drill
A South Vietnamese Aircraft
flying at low level passed by us
about a 100 yards off the port bow
Treetop tall and put us all on edge

Me

November 1968
USS Iwo Jima LPH-2
Westpac
South China sea
Just off the coast of Danang

While I wasn't looking for it
I found a photograph of me in the war online
I was standing next to my crashed helicopter
In a hot LZ
I never look at such things
they hold too many bad memories
I gasped and sobbed a bit
for the scared young man in the photo
He has no idea what fear is yet
and how difficult life will become
and what the difference is between
living and dying
and how many fractions of inches
make up that difference
along with the luck of the draw
In the few short hours until nighttime
his life will be forever altered
and his thought process forever changed
as he is plunged into the depths of hell

Ronald J. Whittle

A lifetime resident of Massachusetts, was
born in Worcester and raised and educated
in his hometown of Shrewsbury. Further
education came by way of the U. S. Navy,
Vietnam, the Apollo 13 recovery team, and
45 years of family living. Ron divides
his time between his home in Worcester
and the shores of Cape Cod. His influ-
ences include Tom Waits, Lawrence Fer-
linghetti, Edgar Allen Poe, Ogden Nash,
Ezra Pound and Rod McKuen. Ron is a
member of the Worcester County Poetry
Association, the Works in Progress/ Outlaw
Stage at the Worcester Artist Group, and
a founding member of Worcester Art Walk,

and a member of the Warrior Writers of Boston.

Ron's first book "Goodbye Again" was given glowing reviews and can be found at Barnes and Noble or on Amazon or his performances. Ron has also appeared on many television programs and he has also appeared at the Massachusetts State Poetry Festival in Salem, Ma, the Great Falls Word Festival and the Garlic Festival in Orange, Ma. Ron has completed a new collection of poems for his next books entitled Hello Again, Once again, and a fifth book in the early stages titled Yet Again.

EPILOGUE

I have often wondered as far back as my time in
Vietnam, if my poetry was just some kind of a sad cry for
help masked under a label of creative expression. I don't
think so, but of course it may well have been. I know, I
had some strange things happen to me over there, that I
cannot explain. I don't know why, but I know Lynne was
with me and protected me from time to time. I could hear
her voice as loud as if she was standing next to me. I
was living in two realities at once, the war on one hand
and with her on the other. Somehow they intertwined to
the point where it would scare me at times. On more than
one occasion, I heard her tell me to do something like
move away from where I was, only to have shrapnel or
automatic gun fire tear up where I had been. I
thoroughly believe she was there in spirit to save me and
I listened to what she said to me and I believe that she
kept me alive. I haven't been able to tell her thank you,
all I have been able to do is document in poetic form
what I saw and did. Only now can I tell her how much
she meant to me. She was everything that was good in my
life and the war, well I'm sure you can imagine how bad
that could get. To this day I have a tough time
remembering those days of desperation but I have found it
soul cleansing to write about them. Lynne, if I never get
to see you again could you answer a couple of questions
before I pass. In that time frame late 1968 through early
1970. Did you ever dream about me or have vivid thoughts
about me? Do you believe in telepathy? I believe there
was some kind of a connection on a level I just don't
understand. I only know for sure that, I believed in you
and still do.

Ron Whittle
Free
War Zone

Made in the USA
Middletown, DE
18 January 2020